THE STRAIGHTFORWARD BUSINESS PLAN

John McCormack

Editor: Roger Sproston

Straightforward Publishing
www.straightforwardco.co.uk

CONTENTS

Introduction

SECTION 1-WHAT IS A BUSINESS PLAN?

Chapter One. The Purpose of a Business Plan   13
What is a business plan?   13
How long must a business plan be?   15
What resources do you need to produce a business plan?   16
Key points from Chapter One   17

Chapter Two. Ten Quick Tips When Writing Your Plan   19
Writing your plan for the reader   19

SECTION 2. SETTING OUT OBJECTIVES AND STRUCTURE/LOCATION OF YOUR BUSINESS

Chapter Three. Setting out Clear Objectives for   23
Your Business and Defining a Business Strategy
SMART Criteria   23
Mission statements   24
Defining your Business Strategy   25
Strategic analysis   26
PESTE Analysis   26
Political   26
Economic   27
Social   27

Technological   27
Environmental   27
Auditing resources   27
Physical resources   28
Human resources   28
Financial resources   28
Evaluation of future options   28
Strategic implementation   29
Planning and allocation of resources   29
The Structure of a business   30
Management of people and systems in a business   30
Business control systems   31
Strategic threats   31
Key points from Chapter Three   33

Chapter Four. Choosing The Structure of Your Business 35
The sole or proprietary business   35
Partnerships   35
The Limited Liability Company   37
Looking at Franchises   38
Advantages of a franchise   38
The disadvantages   39
Different types of franchise   39
Patents and registered designs   40
Patents   41
Registered designs   41
Trademarks   41
Service marks   41
Copyright   42
Key points from Chapter Four   43

Chapter Five. Location/Premises/Employees-Making the Right Choice   **45**

Location of your business   45
Working from home   46
Planning permission   47
Change of use   47
Health and safety at work   48
Inspectors   48
Employing people   49
What are my responsibilities as an employer?   49
National Insurance Contributions   50
Discrimination and the Law   50
Trade unions   50
Tax and national Insurance-more details   50
The law and you as an employer   52
Recruiting and motivating employees-doing it yourself   53
Job centres and employment agencies   53
Training   53
The personal approach   53
Key points from Chapter Five   55

SECTION THREE. SORTING OUT YOUR MARKETING AND PRICING STRATEGIES

Chapter Six. Marketing Your Business   **59**

Market research   59
Marketing generally   63
Advertising   63
Leaflets   64
Directories   64

Advertising in magazines 65
Newspaper advertising 65
Television advertising 65
Radio advertising 66
Using an agent 66
Direct mail 66
Using sales representatives 66
Internet marketing 68
Search engine optimisation 68
Making your site visible to search engines 69
Quality content 69
The use of key words and phrases 69
Search engine marketing 70
Purchasing traffic 72
Email marketing 72
Co-registration 73
Using vouchers and coupons 73
Affiliation 73
Market places (ebay etc) 75
Social media 75
Blogging 75
Key points from chapter Six 77

Chapter 7. Pricing Your Product-Creating a pricing Plan 79
Pricing your product 79
Your costs 79
Example 80
Competitors prices 81
Key points from Chapter Seven 83

SECTION 4. FINANCIAL CONTROL OF YOUR BUSINESS-CREATING YOUR BUSINESS PLAN

Chapter 8. Raising finance   87

Investment of own funds	87
Short-term finance	87
Trade credit	88
Factoring	88
Invoice discounting	88
Long-term finance	89
Business loans	89
Hire purchase and leasing	89
Finance leasing	90
Operating leases	90
Contract hire	90
Soft loans	90
Grants	91
Crowd Funding and peer to Peer lending	93
Key points from Chapter Eight	99

Chapter 9. Exercising Financial Control   101

Profit and loss forecasting	101
Cashflow forecast	101
Preparing a forecast	102
Other Terms	102
Over trading	103
Collecting money on time	103
Check customers ability to pay	103
Set out terms of trading	104
Set up a system	104
Keep clear and accurate records	104

Collect your payment on time 104

What information must be kept? 105

The advantages of a bookkeeping system for
your business 106

How to record the information you need 107

Proprietary systems 107

The analysed cash book system 108

The double entry system 110

Computerised systems 110

Key points from Chapter Nine 112

Chapter Ten. Creating Your Business Plan-Finer Points 113

Constructing the Plan 113

Main considerations 114

Presentation 114

Chapter Eleven-Example Business Plan Template 117

Chapter Twelve Tips When Buying an Existing Business 129

Inspecting a Business for sale 129

Goodwill 130

The process of purchasing a business 131

Conclusion

Useful addresses

Index

**

INTRODUCTION

The latest in the series of publications in the Straightforward Guides series, The Straightforward Business Plan, Revised Edition, aims to give the reader a clear and concise introduction to the various aspects of effective business planning.

This book has been produced with a view to providing the reader with a practical understanding of what is involved in the process of business planning, whether your business is traditional or an internet based business. As such, it is targeted at those individuals and organizations that have no experience of business planning but would benefit from an understanding of these processes.

Organizations which will benefit include; sole traders, partnerships, small companies and voluntary organizations, on the other hand students of business studies and economics will also benefit. The book also aims to provide a comprehensive insight into business planning for anyone hoping to start up their own business.

The book includes invaluable information on setting up a business, employment law, marketing and also finance. There are a number of newer methods of obtaining finance for business. Crowd-funding and peer to peer lending are relatively new and there is also a newer method is financing by internet giants such as Amazon and Paypal. In terms of Amazon funding, a business would need to be trading successfully on Amazon and then would be offered loans, or would apply for a loan, to expand their business. Typically, the current interest rate is 6% .

However, whatever method of trading or funding, in order to create the business in the first place you need to have followed a plan.

A model business plan is included which will help in the initial stages of business growth. You might find it useful to visit either www.bplans.co.uk or www.business-plans.co.uk both of which offer a range of different business plans for a wide variety of business. These will help you to tailor your plan to the business that you have in mind.

The whole process of business planning involves thinking and asking questions, and it is to these questions we now turn. Although most people who are faced with the prospect of producing a business plan, in particular in response to a request from their bank manager, feel daunted, the process is actually straightforward and with the aid of this book the task should be that much simpler.

**

SECTION 1

WHAT IS A BUSINESS PLAN?

- Defining a Business Plan

- Tips on writing a Business Plan

Ch.1

THE PURPOSE OF A BUSINESS PLAN

What is a business plan?

When answering this question, it is tempting to say that a business plan is a document which the budding entrepreneur can present to his or her bank manager, or prospective funder as a means of assuring them of the viability of the proposed business, thereby securing start up funding.

In a sense, this is true. Banks are usually reluctant to finance small business start-ups, simply because so many have gone bust over the last ten years. Moreover, they have done so, according to many economic commentators, precisely because such small businesses have not thought about how it is they are going to survive and prosper in what is almost always a very competitive environment; they have not produced a business plan.

It is, therefore, erroneous to see business plan as simply a tool for negotiation with the bank manager. A business plan is, above all, a strategic document which assists the entrepreneur to think very carefully about all the aspects of the business that they are getting involved in. A good business plan will illustrate detailed research and evidence around such aspects of business as:

• The product/service; what exactly is it? It may be obvious to you, but unless you spell it out it may not be clear to your customers;

- The market; is there evidence of demand for your goods and services? Is the competition fierce? Are you entering a niche market? Is the market prone to fluctuation for any reason?

If so, how do you propose to deal with this?

- Your unique selling point (usp); what is it that makes your goods and services better than those of your competitors? Price? Quality? Anything else?

- Yourself; have you got what it takes to be successful in your line of business? What relevant experience/training have you had? How do you propose to remedy any shortcomings in these respects?

- Business development; what sort of life span are you putting on the business? What are your ultimate business objectives? Growth? Diversification?

- Capital funding; what level of funding, if any, do you need to start up your own business? How much money can you afford to put into it?

- Management and personnel; are you intending to employ other people? If so, what will their roles be? How will they relate to you? Are you aware of the legal and cost implications of employing staff.

- Legal requirements; is your proposed business subject to certain legal requirements, e.g., health and safety legislation, fire regulations, VAT, licensing etc.

- Location and premises; from where do you propose to run your business? Does location matter? What size of premises do you need and what do they cost? Is it feasible and/or desirable to work from home?
- Budgeting; what are your overheads and likely level of income? Is there any scope for price variation in order to cope with increased competition?
- Cash flow; at what points in the year will you face big bills? When can you expect an upturn in sales? What level of overdraft, if any, will you need to service the business?

These are the key questions which any good business plan will address, and it is the process of answering them-and thinking about them-which is most beneficial to the entrepreneur.

How long must a business plan be?

There are no golden rules regarding the length of a business plan. Always, the most important aspect of the plan is the quality of research, evidence and information provided. Needless to say, however, if a business plan purports to cover a long period of time, 10,20, 30 years for example-it will inevitably entail the provision of more information, thus elongating the size of the document.

Large businesses sometimes have business plans which cover a period of up to 30 years. Small businesses, if they have a business plan, normally cover a period of 2-3 years. In the case of new businesses, it is sometimes a good idea to have a business plan for the first year of trading only, to "test the water" and to review the plan at the end of the first year, producing what might be a more realistic 2-3 year plan, based on the experiences of the first year.

As a rule of thumb, however, a business plan should aim to be around 10-12 sides of paper in length, with relevant appendices attached (cash flow forecast, profit and loss forecast, budget calculations etc)

What resources do you need to produce a business plan?

Large companies producing 20-30 year business plans employ highly qualified accountants and financial experts with highly sophisticated computer equipment to assist them in the drafting of their business plans. As a consequence, the small independent trader may feel somewhat ill qualified to produce such a plan. However, it is possible to produce a business plan without expensive equipment and expert advice. In particular, because the proposed business is small, there are less complications which experts would normally deal with.

A business plan can be produced by a small trader if he/she has the following resources and assets:

- time
- commitment
- numeracy
- literacy
- patience

These are all the human resources required to produce a business plan. The only other things needed are a pen and piece of paper!

Now read the key points from Chapter 1.

Key Points from Chapter 1

■ A Business plan is a strategic document which assists the business person to think very clearly and carefully about all aspects of the business they are involved in, or getting involved in.

■ A good business plan will illustrate detailed research and evidence around all aspects of business.

■ A good business plan will help you to understand your unique selling point as a business.

■ There are no golden rules regarding the length of a business plan.

■ A business plan can be produced by anyone with basic resources.

**

Ch. 2

Ten Quick Tips When Writing Your Plan

Before we look at setting out clear objectives for a business, there are a few pointers which should be followed when producing a plan. Many of these are covered in the following chapters.

Writing your plan for the reader

The starting point for any business plan should be the perspective of the audience. The questions that you need to ask yourself are:

- What is the purpose of the plan-is it to obtain funding, for example? An investor will need clear answers to their questions, such as will they get a return on their investment.

- Have you carried out market research-is your plan detailed enough-without this detail your plan will not clear the necessary hurdles.

- Do you understand the competition?

- Is the plan detailed enough? Business plans should ensure that the reader has enough information to make decisions on whether to fund you, or whatever it is that you are asking them to do.

- Focus on opportunity-if you are seeking investment in your business it is very important to describe the investment opportunity. In short, why should an investor choose your business over and above others.

- Ensure that you cover all key areas in your plan-you should undertake research on what a plan should contain-books like this will go a long way to helping you. However, it does no harm to obtain as much specialist advice as possible.
- Do your sums-when you are outlining the costs involved you should pay as much attention as possible to detail. Potential investors, whoever they are, will turn away if the figures do not stack up.
- Create an executive summary-one of the most important components is the executive summary of the business plan. This is a summary of the entire business plan and is usually contained at the start of the plan. If investors like it they will read on. If not they will pass. If there is no summary they will probably not even consider it.
- Review the plan-once you have completed the plan have it independently reviewed. Select a person detached from the process.
- Implement the plan-a plan should always be viewed as a living document and contain specifics regarding dates, deadlines and specific responsibilities.

Now turn to Section 2.

**

SECTION 2

SETTING OUT YOUR OBJECTIVES AND COMPANY STRUCTURE/LOCATION

- Setting Out Clear Objectives

- Defining Your Strategy

- Deciding on The Structure And Location Of Your Company

Ch. 3

Setting out Clear Objectives for your Business and Defining a Business Strategy

---

Before we look at the variables that should be entered into a business plan, we should look generally at the management of a business. In this chapter we will look at the process of setting objectives for a business, i.e. what are your aims and goals. We will also look at the development of a business strategy.

It is absolutely essential to have a crystal clear idea of what the main objectives for your business are. Business objectives relate to a business as a whole and to what you want to achieve in the long and short term. Short-term objectives will relate to what you want to achieve on an annual basis, over a period of twelve months. Long-term objectives relate to a period (usually) of five years.

It has become commonplace now to set up a criteria against which you can measure the effectiveness of your business objectives. This is known as 'SMART' criteria. Within SMART all the objectives that you set for your business must be:

- Specific
- Measurable
- Agreed
- Realistic
- Timed

The above are self-explanatory and enable a business owner to set clear objectives which can be re-evaluated over time. SMART objectives should be set against a clear MISSION Statement.

Mission statements

The best way to quantify business statements is through a mission statement. The mission statement is really a vision statement which details the whole point of your business. There are four key components of a mission statement which must be succinct and clear:

- The role or contribution that a business makes-what exactly are you in business for?
- A definition of the business-this should be given in terms of the benefits you provide or the needs that you satisfy. It should not define what you do or what you make.
- An outline of your distinctive competencies-the factors that differentiate your business from the competition. These are the skills and capabilities that are offered by you as opposed to other business in the same field
- The indications for the future-what the business will do in the future, what it can realistically achieve.

A clear and coherent mission statement is written in two parts. In the first part you will outline the industry that you are in and the products that you offer. The second part comprises the business strategies that you will follow to achieve success.

A few examples might be:

- We will provide a first class service to all customers
- We will achieve high productivity levels through sound planning, organisation and teamwork
- We will generate sufficient profits to ensure ongoing investment in the business
- We will earn high employee loyalty and motivation by respecting their capabilities and their motivation and providing training opportunities
- We will gain recognition in the market for being a highly professional, ethical, quality assured business.

Obviously, the above needs to be fleshed out and thought through but it is the basis upon which the operations of your business will be founded and on which the SMART objectives will integrate in order to ensure that the business moves forward and achieves its goals.

Mission statements need to be re-evaluated on a regular basis as there is always the ever-present danger that it will become just a form of words that sounds good but has no bearing in reality.

Taking SMART objectives and Mission Statements further, basic marketing objectives should mesh with both. We will be looking at marketing later in the book.

Defining your business strategy
As the owner of your business, or one of the owners, you will be responsible for defining business strategy. Strategic management, essentially, has three components:

- Analysis-where are you now and where do you want to be?
- Choice-what options are available to you?
- Implementation-implement your strategy based on the analysis and options.

Strategic analysis

There are two distinct areas of any business that require analysis:

- The environment
- The resources of the business

PESTE analysis

There are a number of factors in the environment that can have an impact on your business. The PESTE analysis enables you to focus on these.
PESTE stands for:

- P = Political
- E = Economic
- S = Social
- T = Technological
- E = Environment

Political

When examining the effect of political forces on a business we are really referring to legislation which has a direct impact on business, such as health and safety legislation and employment law. It is necessary to comply with all legislation and to be seen to be doing so.

Economic

Economic forces will include all the variables that may have an effect of the profitability and sustainability of your business. These can include, inflation, interest rates and, if you trade abroad, interest rates. Changes in the budget will also, invariably, have an effect on you.

Social

Social forces can be complex and include demographic changes that will affect your business. For example, if you sell shoes, the fact that there is a falling birth rate in a particular part of the country may affect demand, will affect demand, for the type and size of shoes needed over the longer term.

Technological

The rapid changes in information technology and relevance to all businesses must be taken into account when devising future strategy.

Environmental

The impact of business on the environment must be evaluated and taken into account when formulating any business strategy.

Auditing resources

Having considered the business environment through PESTE, we should now look at auditing the resources of the business. If the business is new then an analysis of what resources might be required to achieve your aims will be necessary. There are three main headings under which your resources will fall:

- Physical resources
- Human resources
- Financial resources

Physical resources

Physical resources include plant, machines, tool, vehicles and so on. An audit of these resources whether existing or needed in the future will include longevity, cost of future replacement and also maintenance.

Human resources

This will be an assessment of staff needed in the future, if you are a new business, or existing staff if you are established. An audit of human resources should take into account staff development, which will be based on the future skills requirements of staff allied to your own strategy for the business. We will look at staff later in the book.

Financial resources

This area, like the other two, is of vital importance. Without financial stability the business will not survive. An audit of financial resources will include all the sources of finance that you have. This audit will also include an analysis of debtors and creditors. The end result should be a clear determination of current and future viability and, if problems are identified, the rectification of these problems.

Evaluation of future options

The next step in the process, after completing the analysis of your business, is the evaluation of all the different options that have been thrown up. This evaluation has to be alongside the business goals and objectives previously set. Generally, when assessing options, there will be four available:

- Consider withdrawing from the market completely
- Consolidate the existing position within the market
- Increase market penetration
- Introduce new products or services.

The above will clearly emerge following your analysis of the business. Withdrawing from the market can mean liquidation or sale of the business. Consolidation is usually an internal process where the business may concentrate on overall efficiency. Increased market penetration essentially means expanding into new markets for existing products and services. Introduction of new products and services can mean adapting the existing technology or products to suit new markets.

Strategic implementation

There are two aspects of implementation that you need to consider. One is planning carefully the other is the actual implementation. There are three key areas into which you can break down the implementation process:

- Planning and allocation of resources
- The structure of the business
- Management of the people and the systems in the business.

Planning and allocation of resources

The resources of a business, as we have seen, are physical, human and financial. For a new business it should be fairly easy to plan what resources are needed and then allocate them. However, this is more complex for a growing business. The planning of physical and human resources will be easier than the planning of financial resources. We will look at financial forecasting later on in the book.

The structure of a business

Again, if the business is new the structure is likely to be less complicated than a growing business. Initially, in a new business, management can be hands on. In a growing business management will need to be delegated. This will involve a clear idea of the direction of the business, of the integration of different tasks. It is, however, very important that the owner of the business has complete financial control.

Management of people and systems in a business

If it is necessary to employ staff in your business then it is very important indeed that you have staff management strategies in place.

When considering management planning in this area there are a number of considerations:

- What do you want from your staff-what is their function?
- How do you want them to perform-to achieve the task in hand?
- When do you want them to perform?
- What will be the salary structure and overall cost?

- What training will be provided to enable them to perform and to achieve greater job satisfaction?

The question of staff management and motivation, and the meshing of all the tasks to produce satisfactory outcomes is one of the most difficult areas of business management, next to financial management.

Business control systems

Integral to all businesses is the need for a management information system. This will enable you to control your business effectively. The main areas where you will need an information system are:

- Financial performance-the ability to analyse how the company is doing and where it is going in the future
- An ongoing analysis of the marketplace
- A sales and distribution analysis
- A Physical resource analysis
- Human resource analysis.

The above are not exhaustive but are the key indicators from which you can draw information to enable you to manage the business in the present and the future. We will look at management systems later in the book.

Strategic threats

In business, there are ever present threats to the viability of your business, to your market share. These can be from new entrants into the market place, i.e. new companies, the threat of other products (substitute products), this could be an imitation of your product but cheaper, the power of suppliers and buyers, effectively the ability to create monopolies and control prices and competitive rivalry from other companies.. These factors need to be analysed on a regular basis because if they aren't then you will find yourself at a sudden disadvantage.

Now read the key points from Chapter 3 overleaf

**

Key points from Chapter 3

■ It is absolutely essential to have a crystal clear idea of what the main objectives are for your business, both short and long term

■ Business use the SMART criteria within which to set objectives

■ Mission statements are essential for business

■ Businesses also carry out strategic analysis using PESTE analysis

■ It is necessary to carry out an audit of resources of your business to give you an idea of what will be needed in the future

**

Ch. 4

Choosing The Structure of Your Business

There are various structures within which your business can operate and it is essential, when formulating your business plan that you understand the nature of each structure.

The sole or proprietary business

This is a business owned by one person. If you are operating alone then this may be suitable for your purposes. The person and the business are legally one and the same. It does not matter what or who you trade as the business is inseparable from yourself, as opposed to a limited company, which is a separate entity. All financial risk is taken by that one person and all that persons assets are included in that risk. The one big advantage is that all decisions can be taken by the one person without interference.

A second advantage is that the administrative costs of running a sole business are small, if your business is VAT registered then you will need to keep records, as you will for Her Majesty's Revenue and Customs. However, there are no other legal requirements.

Partnerships

Partnership is a business where two or more people are joined by an agreement to run that business together. The agreement is usually written, given the potential pitfalls that can arise from a partnership.

Liabilities which may arise are shared jointly and severally and this should be made clear to anyone entering a partnership. Even if you only have 1% of the business you will still be responsible for 100% of the liability. All personal assets of each partner are at risk if the business fails.

Decisions are taken jointly, as laid down by the partnership agreement. If the agreement lays down that partners have differing decision making capacity dependent upon their shareholding then it could be that, in a three way partnership, the decision making process may be hampered because a decision cannot be reached unless the major investor is present.

It is very important indeed to consider the nature of the agreement that you are entering into and it may also be advisable to take legal advice. Partnership usually reflects the way that business was capitalised although other factors may be taken into consideration. For example, an expert in a particular field may join with an investor to create a 50/50 partnership.

It is very advisable indeed to consider carefully the ramifications of entering into a partnership. Many such arrangements end in tears, with both partners hostile to each other. Personal bankruptcy can occur as can the ruin of the partner(s). Profits are usually shared between partners in accordance with the terms in the agreement.

The Limited liability company

This type of company has evolved over the years and provides a framework within which a business can operate effectively. A limited company is usually the best vehicle for business, in all but the smallest of business. It is certainly the only sensible answer if capital is being introduced by those who are not actively involved in running the business (shareholders).

Shareholders inject capital and receive a return (dividend) in proportion to the capital they invest. They are eligible to attend an annual general meeting to approve or otherwise the way the directors are running the business. Annual General meetings also determine how much of the profit will be distributed to shareholders.

Voting is in accordance with the number of shares held and the meeting can replace all or any of the directors if a majority are dissatisfied with them. Shareholders can, if a majority request, call an Extraordinary General meeting to question directors about performance, outside the Cycle of Annual General Meetings.

Control of the company is in the hands of directors who are appointed by the shareholders to run the company on their behalf. The company is a legal entity in its own right and stands alone from the directors and shareholders, who have limited liability.

When a company is created it will have an "Authorised Shareholding" That specifies the limit of a shareholders liability. If all shares have been issued then shareholders are not liable for any more debts that the company may accrue.

Looking at Franchises

A franchise is a business relationship between the franchisor who has a tried and tested business concept and the franchisee who will purchase the right to operate this business. A Franchise will involve a capital investment and payment of ongoing royalties or management fees based on sales-turnover or as a mark up on goods supplied for resale by the franchisor.

Advantages of a franchise

The main advantage of buying a franchise is that you will be buying a tried and tested business idea. Although usually not cheaper than starting your own business you are cutting out all the steps to achieving brand recognition. There are lots of benefits to buying a franchise, the main ones being:

- You will be purchasing a business concept that has been tried and tested in the marketplace
- Lower risks in initial set-up
- Business premises will all comply with a blueprint, which satisfies all regulations
- Publicity and ongoing marketing will be supplied by the franchisor as will training and education in the business field
- Networking opportunities will be available with other franchisors
- You will be operating in a defined geographical area.

In addition to the above, gaining funding to start a franchise is a good deal easier (depending on the franchise) than a start up business. In some circumstances, the franchisor may be able to offer funding for the franchise start up.

The disadvantages

Like most things in life, there are down sides. Once a franchise is purchased, it can be difficult to dispose of it as there are often terms imposed as to resale. Disputes can arise as to the royalty or management fee and there is also the possibility that the franchisor may fail leaving you with a business that may not be viable in isolation.

Different types of franchise

There are franchising opportunities available for all sorts of businesses. In order to assess whether a business is suitable for franchise there are a number of factors which you need to consider:

- The main one-the original business concept must have been tried and tested and proven to be a success.
- The franchise must have a distinct brand image and tried and tested methods
- Operation of the franchise must be profitable and provide the franchisor with a limit

If you look in some popular papers, such as Daltons Weekly, you can see a whole proliferation of business that are for sale as so-called franchises. It is, or should be immediately obvious, that such businesses are highly suspect. It is necessary to look at the characteristics of a business for sale to gauge whether or not it is suitable for franchise. These characteristics will include:

- Products that have a very short life span in the market
- Businesses with minimal profitability

- Business with repeat business based on loyalty to an individual rather than a product or service
- Businesses that are specific to one geographical area.

There are three types of franchise:

- Job franchise-where effectively you are purchasing a job for yourself. These franchises will be one-person businesses and will require you to invest up to £20,000. Examples range from carpet cleaning to vehicle repair.
- Business franchise. Somewhat more complex as these involve the purchase of a complete business with staff. These types of franchise can cost up to £100,000. Such franchises will include fast food outlets and print shops.
- Investment franchises. These are at the top end and usually include hotels and restaurants and a substantial investment will be required, often up to £1 million.

Beware when entering into a franchise. As mentioned there are many 'scams' out there. It is highly advisable to go to one of the franchising conferences, held in the main cities, in order to gain a better idea of what the franchising world is all about.

Patents and Registered designs
In order to grow, industry must continually create and develop new ideas. Innovation is expensive and innovators need protection, to ensure that others cannot pirate their ideas. All of the above items are known as "intellectual property" and, with the exception of copyright, in order to register and protect your intellectual property, you need to contact the patent office. Their

address can be obtained from the Chartered Institute of Patent Agents, whose number is at the rear of this book.

Patent

If you or your company have produced what you consider is a unique product or process, it is very important to register it as soon as possible, before disclosing it to anyone.

The granting of a patent gives the patentee a monopoly to make, use or sell an invention for a fixed period of time. This is currently a maximum of twenty years.

Registered designs

This involves registering what you consider to be a new design. The proprietor must register before offering for sale in the U.K the new design.

Trademarks

A trademark is a means of identification-whether a word or a logo-which is used in the course of trade in order to identify and distinguish to the purchaser that the goods in question are yours. A good trademark is a very important marketing aid and you are strongly advised to register it.

Service marks

This register extends the trademark to cover not only goods but also services. If you are running a hotel for example, you can now register your service mark if you have one.

Copyright

Unlike the other four categories, copyright is established by evidence of creation, and protection is automatic. To safeguard your position, it might be sensible to deposit your work with your bank or your solicitor or send a copy of your work to yourself by registered post. It should be noted that there is no copyright attached to a name or title, only the work itself.

Having given thought to the likely structure of your business, and also factors such as intellectual property we need now to consider, in chapter four, the right location for your business and also questions relating to the employment and management of staff.

Now read the key points from Chapter 4

** **

Key points from Chapter 4

■ There are a number of structures within which your business can operate and it is vital that you find the correct one for you.

■ You can operate as a sole trader, partnership, limited company, or franchise.

■ You should consider areas of patent and copyright that may affect your business.

**

Ch. 5

Location/Premises/Employees-Making the Right Choices and Decisions

Location of your business

To be within easy reach of your customers may be vital or it may be totally unimportant. If you have a retail business, location is a major consideration. If you are in mail order or operate an internet based business, you can operate from anywhere in the country so far as your customers are concerned. If you are a wholesaler, do you require a showroom? If you are operating a factory, do you anticipate the requirement for a factory shop? Is it simply a question of being conveniently located for your customers or are you relying on passing trade? It is vital that, in assessing the right location, you first clearly define the extent to which you need to make yourself accessible to your customers.

In an ideal world, you should be looking to acquire the right accommodation for your scale of operation today and for your expansion plans this year, next year and some years in the future. This applies whether you are looking for a shop, an office, a workshop or a factory unit. Before you start looking for new premises, work out carefully just what it is you need now.

The important questions to consider are:

- How many square feet of offices/storage space/workshop/showroom?

- How many square feet of employees facilities?
- How much car parking space?
- How much outside storage for deliveries, storage and packing?

If you are uncertain as to what precisely you need, or you feel that the shape of your business is going to alter substantially and in the short term, do not commit yourself to a hefty purchase, or even as much as a five year lease. Go instead for a temporary solution, while you determine what your long-term requirements are likely to be.

Never enter into a lengthy commitment unless you feel that the premises are likely to suit you in the long term. Whether you are buying a freehold or acquiring a lease, take independent professional advice on the value. Hire a surveyor who will tell you whether the asking price or rent is fair. Whatever your business, the cost of your premises is going to represent a major overhead. If you get it wrong, you will go out of business.

It is essential to establish that not only can the property be used for the purpose for which we want it, but also that the planning consent will cover any future business development.

Working from home

Particularly if you are starting a new business, maybe an internet based business, the idea of working from home is attractive. It enables you to keep your overheads to a minimum, allows you to work the long hours necessary in the establishment of a business, and leaves your options open-if the business does not work out, you are not committed to an industrial property.

It needs to be recognized, however, that working from home can cause considerable problems.

Strictly speaking, if you plan to run a business from home, almost certainly you will need approval or permission either from someone or some authority. There are two kinds of restrictions which may affect your ability to run your business from home. The first is a series of contractual relationships which you may have already entered into, such as a tenancy or lease. The second is that imposed by local authorities-planning, highways, health and safety.

However, if your business is internet based and you are carrying no stock then you may not be affected by these restrictions.

Planning permission

If you want to make a significant alteration to your house in order to accommodate your business, you will need planning permission or building regulations approval. This includes building an extension, loft conversion, in fact almost anything except extremely simple alterations

Change of use

Local authorities state that consent has to be sought for any change of use. The interpretation of change of use is difficult but what you have to decide is whether what you wish to do constitutes a genuine material change of use of the building. You should make sure that you have insurance to cover your business activity within your home. If you have an accident which occurs as a direct result of your business then your insurance will not cover it.

Health and Safety at work

Whatever your position in relationship to your premises, i.e., leasehold or freehold, under the terms of the Health and Safety at Work Act 1974, you have certain obligations to protect yourself, your staff, your customers and your suppliers. Health and Safety Legislation is very important and attention should be paid to it.

Inspectors

There are two types of inspector-local authority inspectors and fire authority inspectors.

Local Authority inspectors are concerned with premises where the main activities are:

- The sale or storage of goods for retail or wholesale distribution.
- Office activities
- Catering Services
- Provision of residential accommodation
- Consumer services provided in shop premises
- Dry Cleaning in coin operated units in launderettes
- The keeping of wild animals for exhibition to the public
- Fire Authority inspectors

The fire authority requires that a place of work should have a fire certificate, and in order for your business to get a fire certificate, the premises need to be inspected. The fire authority will wish to see that there is adequate provision for a means of escape in case of fire, and the necessary amount of equipment. The Fire inspectors will advise you whether these facilities are inadequate, tell you how they can be put right and then re-inspect the premises when you have carried out the necessary work.

Employing People

At first you may be able to run your business by yourself or with help from your family. But if not, as your business expands, you may need to employ people. Before doing this, some businesses may consider it worthwhile subcontracting work. This may be more cost effective in ironing out short term trading highs and lows. However, if you do need to take on employees, then you must do certain things.

What are my responsibilities as an employer?

You must give every employee a written statement of terms of employment. At the time of publication, by law, all employees working 16 or more hours a week must be given a written statement of terms after they have worked 13 weeks in the job.

This statement must include the following:

- name of employer
- name of employee, job title and description
- hours of work
- pay details, including how often the employee is paid
- holidays
- grievance procedures
- sickness and injury procedures
- pension schemes
- length of notice needed to end employment
- disciplinary rules, including dress and behaviour

National Insurance Contributions

If you employ anybody, either full time or part time, you must take tax and national insurance contributions (NIC's) from their wages, and you must also pay the employers share of the NIC's, always consult your local contributions agency office. There are different tax and National Insurance Rules depending on your circumstances.

Discrimination and the law

It is against the law for an employer or a would-be employer to advertise a job that in anyway discriminates against race or sex. After taking on an employee, the anti-discrimination laws still apply to all other parts of the employees job, including wages and holidays.

Trade Unions

Make sure that you know about the various laws which safeguard your employees rights to choose whether to join a trade union.

Tax and National Insurance-more details

Once you regularly employ people, you are responsible for deducting their income tax and National Insurance Contributions, and paying your own employers NI contributions.

When you take on someone, you need to tell your local tax office. You will be sent documents which will show you how much you need to take out of each employees wages, and where to send the money. You must record each employees earnings and tax and National Insurance Contributions, and tell your local tax office about these amounts each year.

In the case of National Insurance, the contributions for your employees will be in two parts. You must pay one part and your employee will pay the other. These contributions depend on how much you pay your employee. HMRC will collect them at the same time as they collect any tax. For more advice on National Insurance go to:

www.gov.uk/government/organisations/hm-revenue-customs. This is the Gov.uk site dealing with NI enquiries.

Your personal insurance depends on your circumstances. If you are a company director, you will be treated in a similar way to your employees. You will be classed as an employee of your company and will pay contributions in the same way as your employees. But, there is no special way to assess directors National Insurance.

You should contact the Contributions Agency Office for advice on this matter. If you are a sole trader, or partner, your contributions will be charged at the same rate each week. You must pay them every month by direct debit or every three months when you receive a bill. You may also have to pay an extra contribution for any profits your company makes. This is assessed and collected along with Income tax.

You should tell the contribution's agency office as soon as you become self- employed.

The law and you as an employer

Having considered some of the main issues involved in employing people, you may want to become more acquainted with the following issues and how the law deals with them:

- terms of employment
- redundancy
- insolvency
- pregnancy
- suspension on medical grounds
- sick leave
- health and safety
- union membership
- itemised pay statements
- continuous employment
- time off for public duties
- unfair dismissal
- rights on ending employment
- union secret ballots
- limit on payment
- race discrimination
- sex discrimination
- equal pay
- disabled workers
- picketing
- Pensions (Automatic Enrolment of Employees)

Although all of the above areas may not affect you, particularly in the early stages of development, if you do intend to employ staff then you should at least acquaint yourself with the areas.

Recruiting and motivating employees-Doing it yourself

You can do your own recruiting by advertising locally or in appropriate papers. Or you could write to colleges and schools for candidates.

Job centres and employment agencies

The Job Centre, the Job Club, or the local careers office are all in business to fit people to jobs. Job Centres or careers offices give their services for free, but an employment agency could cost you as much as 20% of the employees first years salary.

Training

Training is necessary to make sure that staff know why and how a job has to be done. It can also help make them more efficient and help increase their productivity. Investing wisely in staff training pays off in the long run.

The personal approach

The better you treat your employees, the better they will treat you. If you are well mannered, punctual and committed they will be too. Show them that they are valued, encourage their interest in the business and ask them for suggestions. They will probably respond positively but don't be patronising. Have confidence in your workforce and allow them to get on with the job. Checking everything they do creates resentment and not much else. All good managers are able to delegate.

Good delegation is really what management is all about. You could also set targets and give bonuses. This way, you will encourage your employees to work harder. As a result you will increase productivity and waste less time. Payment-you must always pay wages on time and at competitive rates, taking into account the minimum wage and the affordable wage. Show appreciation-praise for a job well done is a real incentive. But try not to be over friendly. This is difficult when you are working one to one, but it might reduce your authority and it will be difficult to take a firm line if you ever need to.

Now read the key points from Chapter 5

**

Key points from Chapter 5

■ The location of your business may be important depending on the nature of the business.

■ When considering premises size and space are key considerations, as is car parking.

■ Depending on your business, it may be possible to work from home.

■ When employing people you will need to be familiar with employment law and also the structure of the various government agencies that exist to help the would be employer.

**

SECTION 3

SORTING OUT YOUR MARKETING AND PRICING STRATEGY

- Working Out Your Marketing Strategy

- Working Out Prices of Your Product

Ch. 6

Marketing Your Business

The next step in formulating our business plan is to look at sales, which in turn means looking at the market and considering the most appropriate form of market research. Sales are vital to any business. Whatever you produce, you must be able to sell. This is necessary in order to survive.

You must be satisfied that there is a demand for your proposed business and you must be able to determine how you can investigate the market in which you want to operate, how many potential clients there are in either the catchment area you operate in or the wider area. If you work in publishing for example then clearly the market for your product would be different for that of a baker or butcher or plumber. A lot of thought needs to be given to this area.

Market Research

The tool that is used to determine demand for a product is market research. Market research can be cheap and simple or highly complex depending on how you approach it and what you might want to find out.

Market research, or effective market research should be able to provide you with information as to what people want and also how much they want and what they will pay for it. Competition which might exist should also come to light. You should not be put off by competition nor should you believe that because there appears to be no local supplier that what you produce will sell. No supplier may mean no demand and competition may mean established demand.

The concept behind all market research is simple, however the practice is practice is often not and unless you have a lot of money the costs may be prohibitive. A good example might be a supermarket. A potential supermarket would want to know concrete facts in order to establish demand. For example, in terms of the percentage of the population, the average number of visits made to a supermarket each year. This they may well be able to establish from their own records if they are part of a chain.

Secondly they would want to know what distance people are prepared to travel in order to visit a supermarket. This will vary a lot but they would be interested in establishing a national average.

With these two facts the supermarket can then establish the catchment area population for the proposed supermarket. Now they need to know something about the competition. How many supermarkets are there in the catchment zone which might have an effect on the proposed supermarket? This is easily established. However, more difficult to determine is the effect on your potential business. If we suppose that the supermarket decides that only 30% of the catchment area is exposed to competition and that they expect that 50% of that 30% would continue to use the supermarkets they presently use. This means an adjustment to predicted customer base.

However, competition comes from other shops not just supermarkets This is why calculations are based on average figures since this additional competition will be fairly standard throughout the country. A survey will be carried out in the locality to check that there are no special factors to consider-special factors which may cause adjustments to the predicted customer base either way.

The next question to be considered is; what is the average spend per visit per customer? Supermarkets will almost certainly be able to answer that one from existing records. From this data, they can predict gross sales and so the net operating profit. If this is not high enough to justify the expenditure, they might be reluctant to proceed with building a supermarket.

The above is a simple model and does not take into account a number of complications but it does give an idea of how market research is carried out. There are two very important factors to be considered-average conditions in the industry and catchment area population, or a knowledge of that population. Although the example given covers selling to the general public the same principle applies when considering selling to other business.

It may be possible to determine industry averages by approaching trade associations. A visit to the bank is also very worthwhile as most high street banks keep statistics which they would be willing to make available. A further source of statistics might be a major supplier in an industry.

Somewhat easier is to determine the magnitude of the target market. Businesses generally fall into one or two categories: those where the customer comes to the business to place the order and those where the business goes to the customer to get the order.

In the first category, the size of your target market will be a percentage of the local population. The size of the population can be found by contacting the records office at your local authority. The percentage which applies to your proposed business will be far harder to determine. The classic method is simple-ask a large enough sample to provide an accurate picture. This is easier said than done. A great deal of research experience is necessary in order to be able to design a questionnaire which can elicit all the right information.

If you can afford it, you could consider employing a market research agency to assist you. If you cannot afford it then you should spend time considering exactly what you want to ask and what you are trying to establish. There are many other places which will hold the sort of information you might need. Your local training enterprise agency (TEC) or the trade association relevant to your business will be only too pleased to assist you.

Once you have established your target market, you might wish to consider exactly how you sell to that market. Easy if you have a shop in the middle of a busy shopping area, at least easier than if you produce books and have to cast your net far wider. It might be useful at this stage to look at marketing in a little more depth.

Marketing generally
You have carried out some form of research and now you are in a position where you wish to bring to peoples attention your product. Obviously different media are more suited to some

businesses than others. Marketing covers a whole range of activities designed to "identify, anticipate, and satisfy customer needs at a profit" (Chartered Institute of Marketing).

Three questions need to be looked at:

- When do customers want needs satisfied?
- How do the customers want the need fulfilled?
- How much are the customers prepared to pay for that fulfilment?

Having found the answers to those questions we have to decide how best to communicate to the target market our ability to meet their needs at a price that they can afford-and communicate that ability to them at a price that we can afford. There are various options that we can consider. However, some of these options are expensive and may well not be within your reach.

Advertising
Advertising takes various forms. It is exceedingly difficult, unless you have deep pockets, to try to deduce the real effectiveness of whichever form of advertising you decide to employ. For example, is it cost effective to spend £800 on a small advert in a tabloid for one day if that £800 could be spent on something longer lasting.

Advertising hoardings and posters are one way. These tend to cover not only billboards but also tubes trains and buses. Hoardings are seen repeatedly by a wide and ever changing audience in the locality of your choice. They are usually inexpensive.

Leaflets

Leaflets can be distributed on a door-to-door basis (either to other businesses or to individual residences) or they can be given to individuals in the street. However, leaflets can also be thrown away as many see them as junk mail. The result is that leaflets tend to have a low strike rate. Leaflets can also be delivered as inserts in magazines and newspapers. Magazines direct leaflets to specific audiences and newspapers to local areas. Both can prove expensive and again will be discarded more often than not.

A more effective use of leaflets is to have them available in places where the target market will see them. The classic case here is for businesses offering non-residential facilities for holidaymakers. These can usually be found in hotels and guesthouses. Another use of the leaflet is that of a poster in a newsagent or on other notice boards. This can be effective when being used to attract a defined group of the population who gather together in one place where leaflets cannot be made available. Universities or schools might be a good example.

Directories

Directories will fall into two categories-local and trade. Local directories such as yellow pages are well known mediums of advertising and they are reasonably priced, sometimes free. However, the effectiveness of such advertising depends on what you are doing and also where the ad is placed. Some businesses tend towards directories such as Thompsons because they have less advertisers and are cheaper.

Trade directories are different by their nature. They are unlikely to benefit new businesses as they can be expensive and are in some cases, nationally distributed. This is of little use if your business is local, of more use if your product is distributed nationally. There are now a number of local area and regional directories, often produced by trade associations. Some are available as a book or on disc for use with computers. Those who subscribe to the disc system often receive monthly or quarterly updates.

Advertising in magazines

Magazines fall into three categories-general national, local or specialist. Magazines tend to be more expensive to advertise ion than newspapers but can be more effective. Magazines have a longer life expectancy than newspapers and are often passed on to other readers. Specialist magazines are read by specific people who may form part of your desired target audiences. It is worthwhile bearing in mind that most magazine are national.

Newspaper advertising

National newspapers can obviously reach a lot of people but also tend to be expensive. They are also of little value to those offering local services. Local newspaper advertising can be more effective and also cheaper. Free newspapers are cheaper but can be less effective as they also tend to be seen as junk mail.

Television advertising

It is highly unlikely that television advertising will be relevant in the early years of a business. To launch a television advertising campaign is very expensive indeed. Therefore, this medium will only be a consideration later on, if at all.

Radio advertising

This form of advertising would only be effective if there are sufficient numbers of listeners in the target market. However, in the right circumstances it can be useful and relatively inexpensive. Timing is very important in this medium as you need to target your slots at the most appropriate times and on the most appropriate programme for your intended target audience.

Using an advertising agent

Whether or not an advertising agency is employed will be a matter for the individual business concerned. This decision is down to cost. All businesses placing advertising should set an advertising budget. It could be that placing part of your budget with an agent proves far more cost effective than designing your own campaign.

Agents are usually good at designing and placing adverts and can negotiate discounts with various media. It is certainly worthwhile consulting an agent in order to get an idea of what they can do for you, at the same time raising your own awareness of the direction you should be taking.

Direct mail

Direct mail falls into two categories: untargeted or blanket mailing or targeted. Targeted mail is usually far more effective as untargeted mail can be very expensive and also wasteful. Existing customers of a business are well defined and easily targeted. The secret with direct mail is to keep it short, simple and do it as often as is necessary.

Using sales representatives or agents

Whether or not you choose to use representatives or agents will depend on a number of factors. Where there are few sales required and the selling of a good is complex there may be the need for a representative. Where the product is simple and can be described in an advertisement or leaflet it is unlikely to be necessary to use a representative. There are two main types of representation, the representative or agent.

The representative is a paid member of staff who may or may not receive a bonus or commission based on results. All the representatives running costs will be borne by the business. An agent is a freelance who meets his or her own costs and is paid only on results. The advantage of using the representative is that he or she uses their entire time devoted to your business and is under your total control. The agent costs little to run. However, he or she is not totally dedicated to your business. If other products are easier to sell he may ignore yours altogether.

As you can see, there are a number of ways to reach your target audience, once that target audience has been defined. A lot of thought needs to be given to market research and marketing. All too often, they are the first areas to go through the window in search of savings or simply because you are too busy. However, well defined marketing can produce a corresponding increase in profits and a clear strategy is an essential part of any business plan.

Internet marketing
Having looked at more traditional ways of advertising a business, all of which are relevant, it is now time to look at the process of Internet marketing. ach business has its own overall budget and also goals and targets. In the ideal world it would be nice to be able to invest in both offline and online marketing. However, the reality for most businesses,

particularly start-ups, is that funds are limited. In this case, it is crucial to understand the techniques used in online marketing.

Search engine optimization

Most users of the internet will begin the buying process with a search engine. Search engines are enormously powerful and therefore it is essential that your website is built, maintained and updated to be both customer and search engine friendly. Effective search engine optimization is about making your website visible to the search engines, primarily Google.

Making your site visible to search engines

Your site has to be seen to be ranked. Google uses software called Googlebot to scan individual web pages on the internet and what it finds has a direct impact on how thoroughly your site is indexed and how it can rank in the natural Search Engine Results Pages (SERPS).

Quality content

Good content is the key to a good website. Good content will sell your product. Good content will mean that more and more users will visit your site and become consumers of your products and services. In addition, if you have good content then other websites will want to link up to your site therefore increasing the flow of traffic. If your site and its content is seen as good by Google then it will be ranked higher. People looking for a specific good or service will go straight to your site, bypassing the competition. However, in order to ensure that this is the case, your site should be well designed and regularly maintained and updated.

A by-product of creating good content on your website is that other websites will want to link to your content. This can only be good because it puts your website in a position of being an authority on your given product or service. It will result in more traffic to your site and will attract the attention of Google, improving your rankings. It is no good developing a site which looks attractive and then not maintaining it or trying to optimize your rankings. This will set you back and if you are relying more on people finding your site, as opposed to the more traditional forms of marketing, then it is essential to have an ongoing plan for updating and promoting your site.

The use of key words and phrases

You will want to find your main, or niche, keywords and concentrate on writing content to exploit the words. Keywords are the tool through which those who search the web find your unique product. If you are selling bathrooms for example you will want to come up with as many associated words as possible such as 'designer bathrooms' or 'Victorian bathrooms' in other words try to differentiate and provide as many entries as possible for the user. To just use the word 'bathroom' will severely limit the access to your own site.

Search engine marketing

SEM, Paid Search or PPC advertising is a broad subject that will require research on your part to ensure that you know what you are doing before you invest heavily.

SEM allows you to display an advert on the Search Engine Results Pages or the Search Engines network of publisher websites which you can target to display only to users searching for specific keywords or phrases related to your business. You control your account totally, from the text or images of the advert to how much you wish to spend.

If you elect to run PPC adverts with Google, then your ads will be displayed above and to the right of the organic or natural search results, i.e. the sponsored area. Google calls its program Adwords, which is where the search engine makes most of its profits. There are a number of reasons why search engine marketing is effective:

- It is quick to get started
- You are in control of what you spend
- Your campaigns give you instant visibility

What Google has done with Adwords is to create an online auction for every keyword and phrase in every language. The more competitive a keyword, the higher the price. This is how Google makes its money. You should start your Adwords campaign with a small budget, dip your toe in the water, to see how you go. Setting up an account is simple enough and you should ensure that you read the help and FAQ's on the site before committing yourself.

Adwords works by charging you a fee every time someone clicks on your advert-the more you are willing to pay in comparison to others bidding for the same keywords and the better your landing page is (Quality Score) the higher up the sponsored links you will be placed. The bigger your budget, the more users will be shown your advert and the more that will click through. As soon as your budget has been spent, your advert is taken off until the next day. This allows you to keep tight control of your marketing spend and allows you to see very quickly if the campaign is working and to measure the return on your investment.

Purchasing traffic

When you enter into Google Adwords or place a banner ad on another website you are in effect buying traffic to your site. There are some unscrupulous companies around that charge you for delivering visitors to your site and then don't deliver.

Legitimate performance marketing companies do exist and they are well aware of the business need for traffic. They are also quite sophisticated and can direct the right sort of traffic to your site. Performance marketing companies invest heavily in building up their own network of users or publisher's websites which they then exploit by showing their advertiser's (your) sales message to their network. By carefully categorizing and segmenting their user base, they can effectively ensure that your pages are shown to relevant users. If someone wants law books for example they will only show your advertisement to those interested in law books.

Depending on the size and nature of the performance marketing company you can specify the countries in which you want your advert to be shown or even the approximate age or gender of the target audience. The more specific your requirements the more you will be charged for the service. However, because it is performance based, you will only pay when the campaign results in a conversion. The following are a sample of companies that offer Performance marketing.

Burst www.burstmedia.com
DoubleClick www.doubleclick.com (Now Google Marketing Platform)
ValueClick Media www.conversantmedia.com

There are many more!

Email marketing

Email marketing is an effective way to send your message before you have had a chance of building up your own database of customers. Performance marketing companies will provide lists that are segmented by interest. You will need to check with the provider that all addresses have been cleared and have given their consent to receive third party promotional emails. I receive many such emails every day which I have not consented to and which I delete, so it is important to do your homework beforehand.

Affiliation (as advertiser)

There are a wide variety of affiliation networks available which marry advertisers to publishers. Most networks charge new advertisers a set-up fee which gives your business access to the network of affiliates. Set-up fees can be hefty so you need to go into this with care. In addition, most networks charge advertisers a monthly fee which covers continued access to the network. Ongoing performance can be monitored through the networks portal and affiliates reports can be generated. The strongest aspect of affiliation is payment on performance. You only pay a commission if your affiliate delivers a lead, registration or sale. You are free to pay as much or as little as you want for each of these conversions. Affiliates take campaigns seriously and invest time, money and effort to promote advertiser's products and services. The relationship is two way and you also have to be serious, keeping them up to date with new products, pricing and any offers or promotions that you intend to run. As with all aspects of business, good communication is the key.

Using vouchers and coupons

The use of vouchers and coupons to promote and sell products, usually at a discount, is becoming increasingly popular with online business. The idea has been around for ever, being used for all sorts of off-line business but it is now being used for online trading. Coupons usually allow customers, whether existing or new, to benefit from a promotion by entering a code online at the point of purchasing. The utilization of the code will modify the customers order in some way corresponding to the offer.

These coupons can be printed and distributed through print media, handed out in the street as a flyer or as part of promotional literature, or through any other medium. They can also be distributed online by adding the coupon to a social media post such as facebook or twitter. They can also be sent to existing customers in a mailshot. The use of coupons as part of your selling strategy will require some work to your site and again this is what you will be asking your web designer to do for you.

Co-registration

Co-registration is a lead and customer acquisition strategy used by numerous brands. It is performance based-you only pay on results. Co-registration involves placing a short text or image advertisement for your company on the registration pages of high volume third party websites or landing pages. Usually, you are sharing the page with other advertisers who sell similar products or services, or the page is themed in such a way as to link the advertisers. This method of promotion allows users to request additional information about your product or service and in turn provides you with their contact details.

Co-registration allows you to build a permission based, targeted database of consumers interested in your service and, depending on the volume of the third party site, allows you to develop lists very quickly.

Rich media

Rich media is, basically, videos, pod casts and other images which will serve to improve your visibility and differentiate you from other sites selling similar products. Most shop windows have excellent displays and lure customers in. Web portals should be the same and a short video can do wonders when it comes to displaying your product, or telling customers more about you and your company and what products or services you sell.

Social media

Social media, such as Facebook and Twitter is now so widespread that it would be foolish not to advertise your existence on their sites. By opening accounts with platforms such as Facebook, Twitter and Linked In you will be able to reach your potential audience and also hear what is being said about your company, product or service.

Blogging

Adding a blog to your business website is a simple procedure for any web developer and the quality and customization options from the big payers such as Wordspace and Blogger leaves very little need to develop your own platform. A blog will allow you to produce articles, presenting news and comment about your business and its operations. Blogging helps to develop brand building and may provide you with competitive advantage..

Market places

Market places such as Ebay can be very useful. Although initially conceived as a site where individuals can buy and sell, it now has a facility for professional sellers. Ebay and Amazon in the UK, and Priceminister and Play in Europe, among a few others, provide online business the opportunity to enjoy a worldwide audience by listing your products or services and offering them to their enormous customer base. By paying a listing fee, or a monthly fee plus a share or percentage of the sale price, your business can gain enormous reach within a very short time.

To make it easy for businesses to sell via marketplace sites, these online sellers offer a route to professional sellers to be able to bulk load their products. This is achieved through XML, CSV or through an online portal. There will be some work involved on your side adapting your product database to the platforms particular product classification rules, but once that is done, it is usually a straightforward process loading your products.

The listing fee, commission on sale and other fees can tend to be high if you are selling low margin items. However, the sheer size of the audience can make it worthwhile. As with many other things, it is a case of trying it, dipping your toe in the water and see whether it is worth carrying on.

Now read the key points from Chapter 6 overleaf.

** **

Key Points from Chapter 6

■ It is vital that you understand the market and the demand for your product.

■ Effective market research, and an understanding of how this works, is vital to your business.

■ Marketing covers a whole range of activities designed to identify, anticipate and satisfy customers at a profit.

■ There are a number of ways of reaching customers to determine demand, advertising, leaflets, television, radio, direct mail and more. You may consider using an agent to help you. The internet is becoming more prominent as a marketing tool.

**

Ch. 7

Pricing Your Product-Creating A Pricing Plan

A well thought out pricing plan is essential to the future prosperity of your business, and will also help you to make the most of your opportunities.

To develop the right pricing plan for your business, you need to start by working out what your costs are. You need to look at what your competitors are charging and try to estimate what your service or product is worth to your customers. By knowing what costs you are incurring, you will be able to work out what your "break even" point is. How much do you need to sell before your business covers all its costs, including your own (essential) drawings, but before it makes a profit. Unless you can identify what your break-even point is, you could operate at a loss, without realising until it is too late.

Your costs

Costs can be divided into fixed (overheads) and variable (direct) costs. Fixed costs include your essential personal expenses, such as Mortgage, food etc, as well as rent, heating and lighting wages and interest charges. They tend to stay the same no matter how much you sell. Variable costs, however, increase or decrease according to your level of sales. The most obvious cost here is the actual cost of materials required to manufacture the product but can include other things such as transport, postage or additional labour. The price you charge for your product has to cover all of the variable costs and contribute towards your overheads.

Outlined below is an example of a break-even point.

Fred Peters Car Wash Limited	Cost per annum
Personal Drawings	£10,000
National Insurance	£294
Tax	£500
Stationary	£100
Advertising	£400
Telephone	£320
Depreciation of van (over 5 years)	£1,000
Petrol	£900
Servicing	£300
Road tax Fund	£130
Insurance	£320
Business Insurance	£140
Materials	£200
Depreciation of equipment	£200
Bank loan £3,000 @5%	£200
Bank charges	£100
Accountants fees	£300
Total	**£15,404**

Fred's essential personal drawings to cover his family expenses is £10,000. He operates a small car wash. He expects to work for 46 weeks a year, allowing for holidays, sickness etc. He estimates that he will work 38 hours per week.

His annual output is therefore:

46 weeks a year Times 38 hours times 0.5 cars per hour = 874

His break even point is:
15,404

874

= £17.62 per car

After researching the market in his area, Fred believes he can confidently charge £20 per car, which will give him a reasonable profit.

Competitors Prices

Unless your service or product is much better than others on the market, you would be unwise to charge a price which is too far above your competitors, as you will find sales very hard too achieve. On the other hand, a low price often implies low quality or low standards.

Competing on price alone is a poor option. It is especially important for small businesses to differentiate themselves by other means, such as personal service, convenience or special skills. Customers rarely buy on price alone and it is worth remembering that you can more easily reduce your prices than put them up. If, when you work out what your prices should be, they do not cover your costs-look again at how you might make your business viable. For example, could you reduce any of your variable costs, could you get supplies more cheaply, can you negotiate a discount or find an alternative supplier? On your fixed costs, could you trim any other expenditure?

Think again about what you are offering. Could it be improved and sold at a higher price? Can you sell different products for more money to increase your profits? Would sales increase if you put up your prices and spent the extra income on advertising and promotion? Every cost incurred in running your business must be recovered either by what you charge for your time, or by the amount you charge for your products. Profits will be made only after all of your costs have been covered. But you may decide to use different prices in different situations. For example, a plumber offering a 24 hour service might decide to charge a premium rate for his services if he is called out during the night to deal with an emergency, a different rate for weekends and another rate for normal working hours.

Achieving a range of prices for the variety of skills offered, taking into account the time you would be likely to spend on each job can give you the flexibility to stay competitive, yet still provide a satisfactory income.

Now read the key points from chapter 7

**

Key points from Chapter 7

■ A well thought out pricing plan is vital to your business.

■ Always take into account hidden costs when pricing goods.

■ Unless your service or product is much better than others on the market, you would be unwise to charge a price which is too far above your competitors, as you will find sales very hard too achieve. On the other hand, a low price often implies low quality or low standards.

SECTION 4

FINANCIAL CONTROL OF YOUR BUSINESS-CREATING YOUR BUSINESS PLAN

- RAISING FINANCE FOR YOUR START UP

- SYSTEMS FOR FINANCIAL CONTROL

Ch.8

Raising Finance For Your Business

Raising finance for your business can be difficult or relatively easy depending on the viability of your business and its ability to meet repayments and also the nature and type of assets that your business owns. It is true to say that raising finance is harder (or as hard) than it ever was. However, you should consider the options below. There are a number of alternatives when it comes to raising finance:

Investment of own funds

At the outset it is almost certain that you will have to invest some of your own time and money into your business. The investment will be financial, i.e. money which is an injection of your own funds into the business. If you are trading as a limited company this could take the form of a loan to the company or share capital. If you intend to operate as a sole trader or a partnership this will be owner's or partners capital.

The non-financial investment will take the form of assets that you already own, such as tools and equipment, or a vehicle. These will need to be valued for inclusion into the firms records and an accountant will almost certainly need to be employed to ensure that they are correctly valued and comply with relevant guidelines.

Short-term finance

This type of finance is usually referred to as working capital finance. It is used to finance working capital and pay creditors and is then itself repaid following receipts of funds from debtors. The most common type of short-term finance is provided by banks in the form of an overdraft.

Trade credit

Obtaining credit from suppliers is also a type of short-term finance. The terms of credit with a supplier will vary according to the type of your business and the particular supplier.

Factoring

Factoring services have been used increasingly by small businesses in the last ten years or so, particularly those businesses who work for large companies or corporations who tend not to pay invoices for up to six months. Factoring enables you to bridge the gap between sending out an invoice and receiving payment. Factoring invoices has the advantage that you can receive immediate payment against an invoice, usually around 80% of face value. It has the disadvantage that there is a cost attached to it and it also has a stigma attached to it and can unsettle those with whom you do business with as it is perceived that you have cash flow problems.

Invoice discounting

This operates on broadly the same principle as factoring but with several differences:

- Control of the sales ledger is retained by you and it will be your responsibility to chase bad debtors, unlike factoring where the bank concerned (usually a bank) will undertake this function

- Because control is retained by you the existence of the arrangement won't be evident to customers

Long-term finance

If the finance is to be used to purchase any fixed asset then you must obtain long-term finance. It is good practice to raise the finance based on the life cycle of that fixed asset.

Business loans

Business loans can be raised from a number of sources. The usual source will be your bank if you already have a business account. Some loans are secured and some are unsecured. With all forms of business loans you need to know exactly what the terms are. Most loans are from £1,000-£1million and are repaid from 1 year to 20 years. You should consider the merits and demerits of fixed rate loans and variable loans. This will be influenced by the economic climate currently prevailing.

Hire purchase and leasing

Hire purchase is a very flexible and relatively easy to obtain form of funding, often used to purchase assets. Leasing is a flexible form of funding. A lease is negotiated with the lessor. Assets that are leased can vary from office furniture to heavy machinery to vehicles. Leasing is distinguished from hiring. Hiring requires the hirer to select an item which is already in stock whilst with leasing an item can be chosen from any manufacturer or supplier. The subsequent lease agreement will be tailor made for the asset involved.

There are three types of lease:
- Finance lease

- Operating lease
- Contract hire

Finance leases

With a finance lease the lessor pays for the asset and becomes the owner. The lessee then pays a hire charge which covers the capital cost of the asset and also interest and service charges. The lessee is responsible for all subsequent maintenance and insurance.

Operating lease

This type of lease is, in the main, undertaken by the manufacturer of products that tend to be highly specialised or technical. The lease will usually provide that the lessor is responsible for all future servicing, maintenance and updating of equipment.

Contract hire

This is similar to an operating lease. One of the most common uses of contract hire is to finance a fleet of motor vehicles. In the case of contract hire, the lessor will take responsibility for all future maintenance and costs, the lessee has only to find fuel costs.

Soft loans

These sorts of loans are available usually on more generous terms and are made through local Enterprise Agencies and are available when conventional funding is not. There are other forms of finance available which would not really be relevant to small business start ups, such as equity finance, where a proportion of the business is given up for finance and venture capital, which is only really for larger investments. It is highly advisable, if you need more detailed advice or assistance concerning finance, that you contact your local business advice centre. These centres are there to assist all potential or existing businesses and will provide someone who is expert in this particular field to advise you.

Grants

If you are looking to secure a small amount of money, a grant or combination of grants may be more suitable for your business. This is one of the cheapest forms of finance but be aware of the non-financial conditions that may be attached to the grant. These could be the number and types of people employed and restrictions on what the money can be spent on. Grants range from local initiatives run by local development agencies to Business Link funding as well as private funds across the country.

Grants and where to get them

There are many thousands of sources of grants and it is not possible to cover them all here. They can, however, be grouped into three categories.

European grants

The European Union is a huge source of funds for businesses of all sizes and the money is usually distributed through the European Commission. This body administers a number of schemes through what are known as Structural funds. There are also specific grant schemes such as businesses involved in agriculture for example. However, at the time of writing we are exiting the EU and access to grants will cease once this takes place.

National government

Grants for small firms come from both the UK government but also the Scottish Parliament, Welsh and Northern Ireland Assemblies. Each of these has its own departments and agencies, which hand out the money based on its own criteria and objectives. There are over one hundred of these bodies but among the most important are:

- Department for Business, Energy and Industrial Strategy
- Department for Employment and Learning
- Department for Environment, Food and Rural Affairs
- Scottish Executive
- Welsh Government
- Enterprise Ireland

Local

In addition to the many local government authorities, there are a number of locally based agencies and organisations which have been established specifically to support and encourage enterprise at a local level. One such example is www.gov.uk which has a grants and support directory where you can search grant schemes by sector or location.

Eligibility for grants

Each grant scheme has its own set of criteria to determine whether a firm or project is worthy of its money. There is no business or industry sector which is excluded from applying for funds. The vast majority of schemes apply without major restrictions but on those that do eligibility tends to fall into three main categories: location; size and industry.

Location-the UK is actually divided up into four countries and in addition to those schemes offered by the UK national government, and those from Europe, each of these four areas has awarding bodies and donates funds to businesses located within their borders. On top of this, there are a number of 'special areas' across the UK which are specified by the awarding bodies themselves and can be drawn up just for one particular scheme.

Certain areas within the UK also qualify for funding because they satisfy criteria for special assistance drawn up by the European Commission on National Regional Aid which breaks down Europe into tiers 1,2 and 3. The main form of aid in these areas is Regional Selective Assistance, a discretionary grant aimed at safeguarding and creating jobs and increasing regional prosperity. However, keep an eye on BREXIT!

As you can see there are a plethora of grants. A good starting point to research grant giving bodies is the Enterprise Advisory Service www.arcweb.com. There are a number of other useful websites such as business link, as detailed above.

Crowdfunding and Peer to Peer Loans

Crowdfunding is a way of raising finance by asking a large number of people each for a small amount of money. Traditionally, financing a business, project or venture involved asking a few people for large sums of money. Crowdfunding switches this idea around, using the internet to talk to thousands – if not millions – of potential funders. Typically, those seeking funds will set up a profile of their project on a website such as those run by our members. They can then use social media, alongside traditional networks of friends, family and work acquaintances, to raise money. Below is a brief description of each of the different type of crowdfunding.

Donation / Reward Crowdfunding

People invest simply because they believe in the cause. Rewards can be offered (often called reward crowdfunding), such as acknowledgements on an album cover, tickets to an event, regular news updates, free gifts and so on. Returns are considered intangible. Donors have a social or personal motivation for putting their money in and expect nothing back, except perhaps to feel good about helping the project.

UK Sites include: www.banktothefuture.com, www.fundit.buzz, www.crowdfunder.co.uk,www.justgiving.com, www.pleasefund.us

Debt Crowdfunding

Investors receive their money back with interest. Also called Peer-to-Peer (p2p) lending, (see below) it allows for the lending of money while bypassing traditional banks. Returns are financial, but investors also have the benefit of having contributed to the success of an idea they believe in. In the case of microfinance, where very small sums of money are leant to the very poor, most often in developing countries, no interest is paid on the loan and the lender is rewarded by doing social good. Sites include:

www.abundanceinvestment.com www.simplebacking.co.uk, www.fundingknight.com, www.trillionfund.com

Equity Crowdfunding

People invest in an opportunity in exchange for equity. Money is exchanged for a shares, or a small stake in the business, project or venture. As with other types of shares, apart from community shares, if it is successful the value goes up. If not, the value goes down. Sites include:

www.crowdcube.com, www.downingcrowd.co.uk, www.seedrs.com, www.propertypartner.co

Borrowing through a Peer to Peer Platform

Over the last few years a new area of lending has been increasing in popularity – peer to peer, or social lending. The idea is that people who want to borrow money are matched up with those who will lend it.

What is peer to peer lending?

This is a form of borrowing and lending between individuals, or 'peers', without a traditional financial institution such as a bank or building society being involved. If you want to borrow money, the peer to peer websites match you up with people willing to lend it to you. As such, the companies behind these services (called 'platforms') act as intermediaries between borrowers and lenders. They can offer lower interest rates than traditional loans. Whether or not this is the case for you will depend on certain factors such as your credit rating. Some of the best deals are available only if you have an excellent credit history and no previous problems. If you apply for a loan, you'll be credit checked using a credit reference agency and must pass the peer to peer company's own checks.

Pros of peer to peer lending

If you want to borrow some money, peer to peer loans can be cheaper than banks or building societies, especially if you have a very good credit rating. Some peer to peer websites have no minimum loan amount (in contrast to most banks and other mainstream lenders) which might suit you if you only want to borrow a small amount for a short period. They are another option if you have difficulty getting a loan from a bank or building society, depending upon your credit rating

Cons of peer to peer lending

Interest rates of peer to peer loans might be higher than high street banks or building societies, depending on your credit rating. You might have to pay a fee to the platform for arranging the loan, even if it is not fully funded. This can mean multiple fees if you have to apply more than once. You might find yourself unable to obtain a loan if you have a poor credit rating or have managed your finances poorly in the past. You might not have the same protections using a peer to peer platform as if you borrowed in other ways. This varies according to how the loans are drawn up and who the lenders are – for example, whether they are institutional investors or private individuals. Ask the platform how this works and how it differs from a normal loan.

How much do peer to peer loans cost?

The interest rates on the loans vary significantly depending on how much of a risk you're seen as. If you have a very good credit score, you might be able to borrow at an interest rate as low as around 3% but in some cases the rate might be variable, meaning the rate can go up or down each month, so you need to check. If you have a poor credit history, your interest rate could be as high as 30% (or more likely you will be rejected). Peer to peer platforms also generally charge a fee to arrange the loans.

How do you apply for a peer to peer loan?

To apply for a loan go to one of the lending sites and register, select the amount you want to borrow and over what term. Then you can see if you'll qualify for a loan and the interest rate(s) you'll have to pay. Peer to peer lenders normally 'parcel up' the loans between lots of different people.

Depending on your credit rating and the individual platform, you might be offered less than you want to borrow or you might be offered a certain amount at one interest rate and different rates of interest by other lenders.

Rules and regulations

Peer to peer platforms and some individual lenders, are regulated by the Financial Conduct Authority (FCA). That means that if you're unhappy and make a complaint, the business has eight weeks to sort it out. If, after eight weeks, you're still not happy, you can ask the Financial Ombudsman Service (FOS) to get involved. The FOS has official powers to sort out complaints between you and a financial business you're unhappy with.

If they agree that the business has done something wrong, they can order them to put things right. The service is free to use.

The peer2peer Finance Association (P2PFA) is the UK industry body for peer to peer finance and was set up to ensure high standards in this fast growing industry. All members must adhere to the rules and operating principles drawn up by the association.

Things to be aware of when applying for a peer to peer loan

Before choosing to apply for a peer to peer loan, be sure to consider:

- If you default on a peer to peer loan, the company might pass the loan on to a debt collection agency which will chase it on behalf of the lender or lenders. As a last resort, it might go to court.

- Missing payments or defaulting on a loan will affect your credit rating. Once the credit agreement is in place the peer to peer lending website will register an entry on your credit report in the same way as most other loans.

Now read the key points from Chapter 8

**

Key points from Chapter 8

■ Raising finance for a business can be difficult at the best of times. It can also be relatively easy depending on the viability of your business.

■ Funding a business from your own resources, mortgaging property, borrowing from family and friends etc, is probably the safest and easiest way to obtain funds-of course this depends on availability

■ There are a number of other areas of finance, the main one being banks-this is where a coherent business plan is necessary.

■ Once started, other areas of finance can be trade credit, invoice factoring, hire purchase, Crowd funding, Peer-to-Peer lending, lease agreements and so on. All these areas help with ongoing cash flow.

■ There are a plethora of grants available from local and national government and also the European Union, although EU funding will no longer be available following BREXIT.

**

Ch. 9

Exercising Financial Control

In this chapter, we will consider the importance of financial control within the process of business planning. In particular, we will look at profit and loss forecasting, cashflow forecasting, effective bookkeeping, tax and insurance and raising capital for your business.

Profit and loss forecasting

A profit and loss forecast is a projection of what sales you think you will achieve, what costs you will incur in achieving those sales and what profit you will earn. There is an example profit and loss forecast sheet in appendix 1 to enable you to practice.

Having this information down on paper means that you will be able to refer to it, and adjust it as your business develops. Not all the headings will be relevant to you, so don't worry if you leave blank spaces.

Cashflow forecast

A cashflow forecast, as the name suggests, forecasts the changes in the cash which comes into and out of your bank account each month. For example, your customers may pay you after one month, whereas you might pay out for rent or insurance in advance. At the same time, you will have to pay for certain costs such as materials or wages and will need to budget for this.

Preparing a Cashflow Forecast

Remember that a cashflow forecast helps you to evaluate the timing of money coming into and going out of your business. In showing you the "movement" of money it takes full account of the fact that you may often not be paid immediately for work done and, correspondingly, that you may not have to pay immediately for goods and services you acquire.

An important purpose of a cashflow forecast is to reveal the gap between your cash receipts and payments. It will show you whether or not, for example, you might need to borrow, and if so, when you are most likely to require additional funds. It is very common for businesses to need more cash as they grow because of the difference in timing of receipts and payments.

Other Terms

Working Capital

Working capital is the term often used to describe the short-term resources used by the business for everyday trading purposes. This consists of:

Debtors-these are customers you have sold to in credit, i.e., they owe you money.

Creditors-these are your suppliers who you have purchased from on credit, i.e., you owe them money.

Stock-this represents the value of materials you have purchased. They may be purchased for immediate resale or they may be in the process of being converted into a finished article.

Cash-this can either be the amount of physical cash you are holding or it may be money held in a current or bank deposit account.

All of the above have to be carefully controlled if your business is to prosper.

Over trading

A problem common to many small and growing businesses is what is described as "over trading". The more sales you make, the more money you will need to spend on funding material and debtors before you are paid for the sales. If your level of sales becomes too high and you do not have the necessary level of working capital to support it, you may simply run out of cash. This can be disastrous for your business and means that a full order book is not the only thing to strive for.

Even with a profitable business and a full order book, it is imperative to have enough cash available. Extra finance can help your cashflow and make it easier to avoid the pitfalls of over trading.

Collecting money on time

For every day a customer delays payments, your profit margin is eroded. You may have to pay interest charges on a loan or overdraft, when the money owed to you could be earning you interest instead.

Check your customers ability to pay

Before you offer customers credit, check that they can meet their liabilities. You may want to take up bank references.

Set out your terms of trading

Be specific about when you expect payment, for example, 30 days from the date of the invoice and make your customer aware in advance of work that you do.

Set up a system

Set up a system which enables you to issue invoices promptly and shows you when invoices become overdue.

Keep clear and accurate records

Inaccurate invoices or unclear records can be one of the main reasons for customers delaying payments. Make sure you send invoices punctually, to the right person at the right address.

Collect your payment on time

Establish a collections routine and stick to it. Keep records of all correspondence and conversations. Give priority to your larger accounts, but chase smaller amounts too. If regular chasing does not produce results consider stopping further supplies to the customer. If payment is not obtained, don't hesitate to ask a reputable debt collection agency or solicitor to collect the money for you. Your Business activities will consist of selling goods and/or services. At the same time you will have to spend money on behalf of the business, on the purchase or rent of premises, raw materials, equipment, stationery etc. etc. in order to conduct business.

Remember that every business transaction generates a financial transaction, all of which must be recorded in books of account on an on-going basis. It is a fundamental management requirement that this be done on a regular basis, at a minimum once a week. Leave it much longer, and sooner or later an iron law of accounting will come into operation. You will have mislaid a financial record or simply forgotten to request one or issue one. When you do get around to up-dating the books, they won't balance. Unless you can discover the error before the end of the financial year your accountant will be faced with the task of reconciling "incomplete records", which he or she will enjoy because of the professional challenge but which costs you more money for more of his/her time.

What information must be kept?

As a minimum you must keep records of the following: -

i) All the invoices raised (or rendered) on behalf of the business, either when the goods are delivered or the services supplied, or shortly afterwards. An invoice is a legal document and constitutes a formal demand for money. It must provide enough information to identify the business which sent it, who it was sent to, what it is for and whether VAT is payable.

ii) A list of your Sales invoices numbered sequentially.

iii) All Purchase invoices received, and listed i.e. those demands made on your business for the payment of money.

iv) Wages and salaries paid, and to whom; Income tax and NI contributions paid over to the Tax authorities.

v) All chequebook stubs, paying-in slips/books, counterfoils of petty cash vouchers, business bank account statements. Without these you cannot compile your books of account.

vi) A full record of VAT, whether paid by or paid to the business.

The advantages of a bookkeeping system for your business

a) To provide accurate information sufficient to assess whether you are managing the business at a profit or a loss, or whether the business is solvent i.e. is there enough cash available in the business to pay all the outstanding liabilities on demand? The right information of the right kind at the right time is a vital management tool. Good management means making informed decisions of the right kind at the right time based on information that is true and therefore trustworthy.

b) To provide the information required for correct assessments of VAT and Income Tax, so as to avoid financial penalties (and possibly a suspect reputation) for incorrect and/or late payments. HMRC keep records for seven years, and so must you. Your accountant will need the best information in order to minimise your tax liabilities, unless of course you decide to submit a statement of income to your Inspector of Taxes without recourse to an accountant. In any event the Inspector will require a calculation of your Income from the business in the form of an Income and Expenditure Account for each trading year.

c) To monitor the behaviour of the business over time by reference to financial summaries "at a glance". You don't need to remember for example how many meals were served in your restaurant business say in this year compared with last year.

The comparison that matters is the financial one with reference to the value of those transactions.

How to record the information you need

There are basically four methods of bookkeeping. Which one to choose will depend largely on the type and size of business you have established. Take advice from a business adviser or accountant if you are unsure as to which is the best one for your needs.

a) Proprietary systems.

These are best suited for sole traders in cash transaction types of business e.g. jobbing builders, market traders or some small shopkeepers. This type of business requires daily record keeping, often including till- rolls for the cash till and offers a simple method of control over finances. A number of pre-printed stationery systems are available at business bookshops. Select one that allows you enough space to record all that needs recording. Worked examples are set out at the beginning of each book to show you how to keep cash records and the bank position, which can be calculated by following the instructions included.

Cash businesses are more vulnerable than other types for the following reasons: -
i) It is far easier to lose or misplace paperwork. Therefore it is easier to lose control and lose money. Therefore it is more difficult to plan for the future.
ii) It is far more difficult to separate the cash that belongs in the business from the cash belonging to the proprietor.
iii) HMRC pay far closer attention to cash businesses because of the greater scope for "creative accounting" and tax evasion.

To minimise these risks, cash business-proprietors are strongly advised to pay their daily cash takings into the bank by using pre-printed paying-in books supplied by their bank. It is also vital to obtain receipts for purchases made from the takings and to keep them in an orderly fashion.

b) The Analysed Cash book System.

This is perhaps the most common method used by small businesses selling mostly on credit, with perhaps some cash sales. It relies on the Single Entry system of bookkeeping, where each entry is, as the name implies, made once only, and all entries are made in one book, the cashbook. The analysed cashbook is the "bible" of the business. It allows "at a glance" analysis because it is arranged on a columnar basis, showing how much has been received into the business, when and from where, how much of each receipt is attributable to VAT and therefore how much is the net amount belonging to the business. All this information is written up on one side of a pre-printed book, the left-hand page, showing all monies paid into the bank on behalf of the business. On the opposite, right-hand page are set out in separate columns details of what has been spent by the business, in other words, monies paid out of the bank, to whom and when.

See overleaf for example of the analysed cash book.

The analysed cash book

Figure 1: Receipts side of an analysed cash book

| | | | ANALYSED CASH BOOK | | | |
| | | | Receipts | | | |
Date	Details	Receipt number	Amount	Balance b/f	Sale of	Other
1 Jan	Cash in hand	-	1000.00	1000.00		
3 Jan	Grant from donor	500	9500 00			
9 Jan	Grant from					
	Dept. of					
	Health	501	7000.00			
9 Jan	Sale of drugs	502	14.50		14.50	
31 Jan	Total		17514.5	1000.00	14.50	-

See fig 2 overleaf for payments side.

Figure 2: Payments side of an analysed cash book

					ANALYSED CASH BOOK			
					Payments			
Date	Details	Receipt	Amount	Salaries	Rent	Elect	Other	Other
		number					expenses	
3 Jan	Stationery for	1	10.00				10.00	
	office							
5 Jan	Purchase of		650.00					
	medical supplies	2						
7 Jan	Driver 's salary	3	200.00	200.00				
7 Jan	Purchase of drugs	4	3450.00					
31 Jan	Total		4310.00	200.00	-	-	10.00	

c) The System of Double Entry

This method of recording accounts relies on ledgers, or separate books of account for each type of transaction. Far greater detail and control are possible using this system. As well as a cash account there is scope for setting up other ledgers such as the bought ledger for purchases, sales ledger, nominal (or business expense) ledger, salaries and so on. It is much easier to monitor how much has been spent over a period of time on each type of transaction, simply by referring to the particular ledger or account, on each of which a running balance is struck. Every transaction is recorded in the major account called the Cash Account and also in the appropriate subsidiary ledger. In this way the Cash Account acts as a "Control" account for all the separate accounts of the business. The most important feature of this system is the characterisation of all bookkeeping entries as either a "credit" ("he trusts" i.e." the business owes him") or "debit" ("he owes"). The sophistication of this method lies in the use of two entries for each transaction. For each credit entry in the Cash Account there must be a corresponding debit entry for the same amount in a different account. Likewise for each debit entry in the Cash Account there must be a corresponding credit entry in a different account. The key words are "equal and opposite". That way the greatest possible degree of control is obtained.

d) Computerised Accounting Systems

A wide variety of off-the-shelf packages are available, which rely on single or double entry methods. It may be tempting to invest in an accounts package at the outset, especially if you intend to use other computer packages in the business. It would be most unwise to start using such a package without understanding the principles that underlie them. Businesses have failed because of the familiar - "GIGO" - garbage in, garbage out. Money is the lifeblood of the business so don't turn it into garbage by neglecting an understanding of the what, why and how of bookkeeping.

Now read the key points from chapter 9

Key points from chapter 9

■ A profit and loss forecast is a projection of what sales you think you will achieve.

■ A cashflow forecast forecasts the changes in the cash which comes into and out of your bank account each month.

■ It is vital to understand the principle and practice of over trading.

■ You need to keep clear and accurate records at all times.

■ You should fully understand the basic principles of bookkeeping.

* *

10

Creating Your Business Plan-The Finer Points

The following pages represent the basis for your business plan and the various sections relate to the sections of the book. If there are parts which you do not feel are relevant to your business, then you should ignore them.

Business plans can be formulated by those already in business and wishing to expand, or by those who wish to obtain funds for a start up. The ideas gleaned from this book will assist people in formulating any type of business plan.

You should construct your own business plan using the outline below as a guide. By referring to the book and also to the details of your own business you should be in a position to formulate your own plan which will be the complete document for your use, particularly for presentation to your bank manager or to other parties. Remember, it has been stressed throughout the book that an impressive business plan goes a long way towards developing your business and raising the necessary funds to go forward.

Constructing the plan

If you have never written a business plan before, it can be difficult to tell exactly how to go about it. What kind of format should you use, is there an ideal length, how should you order the sections in the plan. There are a few main guidelines which should be followed.

Main considerations

- The language used must be concise and to the point. It should be written in layman's terms and in the third person.
- Each section must stand on its own and clearly define and satisfy its objective.
- All conclusions drawn from facts are to be reasonable and credible.
- Where appropriate, facts should be supported by graphs and charts as this makes the statement immediately more visual.

Presentation

- Choose the right font-don't for example couch the whole plan in a tiny font which people cannot read. The normal font for presentation is Times Roman 12.
- Use single spacing between lines.
- Make sure that it is well laid out with sub-headings
- Page numbering to be consistent-usually on bottom right hand corner.
- Formatting on page numbers must be consistent.
- Bullet point marks must be used effectively.
- The plan should contain enough white space for readability.

Cover/Table of contents

The cover page should detail:

- The name of the business
- The main contact's name
- Full address details
- Type of company

- The clients company logo; and
- Reader confidentiality.

The table of contents should include the executive summary-what is in the plan and any appendices.

In the next chapter is an example of a business plan. You should use this as a model but adapt it how you wish. You may find that some of the sections are not relevant and it will also depend on who you are showing the plan to and for what purpose.

**

Ch. 11

An Example Business Plan Template

Example business plan

(Cover page)

Name of business

_____

Address

_____

_____

Contact name

_____

Telephone Number

_____

Sole Trade
Partnership
Franchise
Limited Company
Start up date
Type of Business

1. Executive Summary of the plan

_____

_____

_____

_____

_____

2. Planning ahead

My ultimate goal is:

_____

_____

_____

_____

I expect to achieve the following over the next few years

Year 1

_____

_____

Year 2

_____

_____

Year 3

_____

3. Marketing

I have identified my market as:

_____

_____

_____

_____

_____

_____

_____

_____

My customers may be described as

_____

_____

_____

_____

_____

_____

_____

_____

_____

4. Product comparison table

_____

_____

My Product	Competitor A	Competitor B

_____

_____

Price

Quality

Availability

Customers

Staff Skills

Reputation

Advertising

Delivery

Location

Special Offers

After Sales Service

My product is special because

_____

_____

_____

_____

_____

5. The main advantages of my product over my competitors are

_____

_____

_____

_____

_____

6. Pricing

Calculating your break even point

Personal Drawings

_____

_____

National Insurance

_____

_____

Tax

_____

_____

Stationary

_____

_____

Advertising

_____

_____

Telephone

_____

Rent and Rates

_____

Heating and Lighting

_____

Vehicle Depreciation

_____

_____

Petrol

_____

_____

Servicing

_____

_____

Road Tax Fund

_____

_____

Insurance

_____

_____

Business Insurance

_____

Bad Debts

_____

_____

7. Premises

My business will be located at

_____

_____

_____

_____

_____

Because

_____

_____

_____

_____

_____

Details of my lease/licence/rent/rate/next rent review

_____

_____

_____

_____

8. Details of key staff (if any

_____

Name

_____

_____

Position

_____

_____

Address

_____

Age

_____

_____

Qualifications

_____

_____

_____

Relevant work experience

_____

_____

_____

_____

_____

_____

Present Income

_____

_____

Repeat as necessary

I will need to buy in the following skills during the first two years

_____

_____

_____

_____

_____

9. I estimate the cost of employing people or buying any services I may need in the first two years

Number of people   Job Function   Monthly Cost   Annual cost

My personal Details

Name

Address

_____

_____

_____

_____

_____

Telephone (home)

Telephone (work)

_____

_____

Qualifications

_____

_____

_____

_____

_____

_____

Date of Birth

_____

_____

Business experience

_____

_____

_____

_____

_____

_____

Courses attended

_____

_____

_____

_____

_____

10. Book-keeping

I intend to keep the following records
(which will be kept up to date by myself/book-keeper/accountant)

_____

_____

Other

Accountant

_____

_____

Address

_____

_____

Telephone

_____

_____

Solicitor

_____

Address

_____

_____

_____

_____

_____

Telephone

_____

VAT Number

_____

Insurance Arrangements

_____

Raising finance

By reference to my profit and loss and cashflow forecast, I need to borrow

Amount £

_____

For

_____

_____

Period

_____

_____

I am investing £

_____

11. I can offer the following security

_____

_____

Ch.12

Tips on Buying an Existing Business

This book has centered around creating a new business. However, you may be in a position where you are thinking of buying an existing business. This chapter offers a few tips on what to look for when buying an existing business.

There are many businesses available for sale in all areas of the market and this is, sadly, an area where many people end up losing out, usually to people or concerns that are trying to offload a business that is failing.

Inspecting a business for sale

If you have identified a business that interests you, it will be necessary to make a number of visits to that business and to carry out a number of 'due diligence' checks. In addition to appraising the business from the standpoint of its operations, such as the flow of customers, attitude of the staff, premises and stock, it is essential that you have a handle on the valuation of the business. Many times business are overvalued and overstate their turnover. It is vital to involve professionals, such as lawyers and accountants at the outset. This may cost but is nothing compared to the cost to you if you buy a business and realise that it is failing.

There will be a number of elements involved in forming the price of a business, such as building and stock. It will be essential to ensure that a correct appraisal is carried out. Are the assets as valuable as they are said to be, i.e. their book value? Is the total turnover accurately stated and is it a realistic appraisal of ongoing year on year turnover. Where are the risks?

You will also need to examine the following:
- Trade debtors
- Trade creditors
- Other creditors
- Any agreements such as hire purchase and leases, including leases on buildings
- Bank loans

Basically you will need to ensure that you are not purchasing a risk and that all agreements in place will apply to you when you purchase a business.

Goodwill

There is usually an amount involved for 'goodwill' in a business. This will be the payment for having built up the business and their brand name and their commercial reputation.

Extreme care should be taken in this area. The owner will argue that they have spent years building up the business. The counter argument will be that benefits have been taken out of the businesses over the years which have been produced by the development of goodwill. A professional appraisal of this area is definitely needed.

The process of purchasing a business

When you have been through the process of due diligence, it will be necessary to employ the services of a lawyer who specialises in the sale of commercial properties. This person will draw up a suitable contract of sale, compile a schedule of assets and liabilities that are to be included in the sale and the agreed valuation, search companies house for details of all existing directors and shareholders and other information and complete the necessary forms to register the transfer.

Although this chapter has been brief, the main message is BEWARE when buying a business and carry out a thorough investigation of what you are buying. Look out for any cover-ups and any likely future risks and make sure, before you enter into the purchase that you are totally committed.

**

CONCLUSION

The aim of this book is to ensure that, having read and understood all the key stages of business development, that you are now in a position to formulate an effective business plan. To many people, the very word 'business plan' makes them very nervous because it means work, often delving into areas that are beyond an individuals control. If you go to a bank manager for a loan, he or she will always ask to see a business plan in order to gain the confidence to lend money. Without a business plan, to the bank manager at least, a person is proceeding in an unstructured way, often taking unacceptable risks, and cannot accurately forecast where the business will be in 6 months or one years time.

It is hoped that, having worked your way through the areas of business development and understood the model business plan laid out in chapter twelve, that you will find the process of planning that much easier. A word of advice: if you are in the process of starting up a business, always plan and plot a way forward that will enable you to see the coming year(s) very clearly. This will be of benefit to both yourself and also those who you wish to get on your side in the future, be it a bank manager or government department.

If you are a business in the process of trading and need a plan, put aside time to do this, it is perhaps the most important element in the business process.

Good luck!

Useful Addresses

Advisory Conciliation and Arbitration Service (ACAS)
Euston Tower, (London Office)
286 Euston Road,
London,
NW1 3JJ.
Tel 0300 123 1100

British Chambers of Commerce
65 Petty France
London SW1H 3QB
Tel 0207 654 5800
Info@britishchambers.org

Association of Independent Business
1st Floor
336 Victoria park Road
London TW3 3TG
Tel 0871 918 6213

British Franchising Association,
www.thebfa.org

Business in the Community
137 Shepherdess Walk (London Head Office)
London N1 7RQ
Tel 0207 7566 8650
www.bitc.org.uk

Business Links
See local phone books or
Small firms and business links
Division
www.businesslink.gov.uk

Department for Business, Energy and Industrial Strategy
1 Victoria Street
London
SW1H OET
020 7215 5000

The Chartered Institute of Patent Attorneys
2nd Floor, Halton House
20-23 High Holborn
London EC1N 2JD
020 7405 9450
mail@cipa.org.uk

Companies Registration Office
Registrar of Companies (England and Wales)
Companies House
Crown Way
Cardiff
CF14 3UZ
DX 33050 Cardiff
Emailenquiries@companies-house.gov.uk
Enquiries (UK) 0303 1234 500
Welsh service welshcoordinator@companieshouse.gov.uk
International +44 303 1234 500

The Cardiff office is open 24 hours a day for the receipt of documents
Contact Centre lines are open between 8.30am to 6pm (Monday to Friday)

Registrar of Companies (Northern Ireland)
Companies House
2nd Floor
The Linenhall
32-38 Linenhall Street
Belfast
BT2 8BG
DX481 N.R. Belfast 1
Emailenquiries@companies-house.gov.uk
Enquiries (UK) 0303 1234 500
International +44 303 1234 500
Opening hours between 9am to 5pm (Monday to Friday)
The office does not have a letterbox for deliveries

Registrar of Companies (Scotland)
Companies House
4th Floor
Edinburgh Quay 2
139 Fountainbridge
Edinburgh
EH3 9FF
LP - 4 Edinburgh 2 (Legal Post) or DX ED235 Edinburgh 1
Emailenquiries@companies-house.gov.uk
Enquiries (UK) 0303 1234 500
International +44 303 1234 500

Opening hours between 9am to 5pm (Monday to Friday)
The Edinburgh office has a letterbox for out of hours deliveries

London office and information centre

Companies House
4 Abbey Orchard Street
Westminster
London
SW1P 2HT
Emailenquiries@companies-house.gov.uk
Enquiries (UK) 0303 1234 500
International +44 303 1234 500
Opening hours between 9am to 5pm (Monday to Friday)
The London office has a letterbox for out of hours deliveries

Confederation of British Industry (CBI)

Cannon Place
78 Canon Street
London EC4N 6HN
Tel 0207 935 8165
www.cbi.org.uk

Forum of Private Business

Ruskin Chambers
Drury Lane
Knutsford
Cheshire WA16 6HA
Tel 01565 626001
www.fpb.org

Health and Safety Executive
hse.gov.uk

Federation of Small Businesses
Sir Frank Whitttle Way
Blackpool Business park
FY4 2FE
Tel 0808 20 20 888

Scottish Enterprise
Atrium Court
50 Waterloo street
Glasgow G2 6HQ
Tel 0300 013 3385

Websites

National Enterprise Network
www.nationalenterpriseetwork.org

National Business Register
www.start.biz

The Princes Trust
www.princes-trust.org.uk

**

Index

Advertising, 5, 63, 65, 120, 121
Affiliation, 72
Agents, 66, 135
Amazon, 75
Analysed Cash book System, 108
Auditing resources, 4, 27

Blogging, 75
Budgeting, 15
Business, 3, 4, 7, 8, 9, 14, 17, 19, 23, 31, 33, 38, 40, 89, 91, 92,
          104, 113, 117, 122, 126, 129, 134, 135, 137,
          138
Business control systems, 31
Business loans, 89

Capital funding, 14
Cash flow, 15
Cashflow forecast, 7
Chartered Institute of Patent Agents, 41
Competitors, 6, 81
Computerised Accounting Systems, 111
Constructing the plan, 113
Contract hire, 7, 90
Contributions Agency Office, 51
Co-registration, 73, 74
Costs, 79
Creditors, 102

Daltons Weekly, 39
Debtors, 102
Department for Business innovation and Skills, 92
Department for Employment and Learning, 92
Department for Environment, Food and Rural Affairs, 92

Direct mail, 6, 66
Directories, 5, 64

Ebay, 75
Economic, 3, 26, 27
Email marketing, 72
Employment agencies, 53
Enterprise Agencies, 90, 138
Enterprise Ireland, 92
Environment, 26, 92
European grants, 91
Evaluation of future options, 4, 28
Executive summary, 20

Facebook, 74
Factoring, 7, 88
Finance leases, 90
Financial performance, 31
Financial resources, 4, 28
Franchises, 4, 38

Goodwill, 8, 130
Grants, 7, 91, 92

Her Majesty's Revenue and Customs, 35
Hire purchase, 7, 89
Human resource analysis, 31
Human resources, 4, 28

Inspecting a business for sale, 129
Intellectual property, 40
Internet marketing, 67
Investment franchises, 40
Investment of own funds, 87
Invoice discounting, 7, 88

Job centres, 5, 53
Job franchise, 40

Large businesses, 15
Leaflets, 5, 64
Legal requirements, 14
Local Authority inspectors, 48
Location, 5, 15, 45, 55, 93, 120
Long-term finance, 7, 89

Magazines, 64, 65
Management, 4, 14, 29, 30
Marketing, 5, 63, 77
Mission statements, 3, 24, 25, 33

National government, 92
National Insurance, 5, 50, 51, 121
National Insurance Contributions, 5, 50
Networking, 38
Newspaper advertising, 6

Objectives, 3, 23
Operating lease, 90
Over trading, 7

Partnerships, 4
Patents, 4, 40
Personnel, 14
PESTE analysis, 26, 33
Physical resource analysis, 31
Physical resources, 4, 28
Planning, 4, 5, 29, 30, 47, 118
Planning and allocation of resources, 29, 30
Political, 3, 26
Presentation, 8, 114
Price, 14, 120

Pricing, 6, 79
Profit and loss forecasting, 7
Profits, 36, 82
Proprietary systems, 8, 107
Publicity, 38

Quality, 14, 120

Radio advertising, 6
Raising finance, 7, 87, 99, 128
Recruiting, 5, 52
Rich media, 74

Sales representatives, 66
Search engine optimization, 68
Search Engine Results Pages, 68, 69
Shareholders, 37
Short term finance, 87
Short-term finance, 7
Short-term objectives, 23
SMART, 3, 23, 24, 25, 33
Social, 3, 26, 27, 74
Soft loans, 7, 90
Stock, 102
Strategic analysis, 3, 26
Strategic implementation, 4, 29
Strategic management, 25
Strategic threats, 4, 31
System Double Entry, 110

Tax, 5, 50, 105, 106, 121, 122
Technological, 4, 26, 27
Television, 6, 65
Trade credit, 7, 88
Trademarks, 4
Training, 5, 53

Twitter, 74

Welsh Development Agency, 92
Working from home, 5
Writing your plan, 3, 19

**

www.straightforwardco.co.uk

All titles, listed below, in the Straightforward Guides Series can be purchased online, using credit card or other forms of payment by going to www.straightfowardco.co.uk A discount of 25% per title is offered with online purchases.

Law

A Straightforward Guide to:

Consumer Rights
Bankruptcy Insolvency and the Law
Employment Law
Public law
Business law
Private Tenants Rights
Family law
Small Claims in the County Court
Contract law
Intellectual Property and the law
Mental health and The Law in the UK
The Rights of Disabled people
the Rights of Disabled Children
Divorce and the law
Leaseholders Rights
The Process of Conveyancing
Knowing Your Rights and Using the Courts
Producing Your own Will
Housing Rights
Bailiff and the law
Being a Litigant in Person
Probate and The Law
Company law
What to Expect When You Go to Court
Guide to Competition Law
Give me Your Money-Guide to Effective Debt Collection

General titles

Letting Property for Profit
Buying, Selling and Renting property
Buying a Home in England and France
Bookkeeping and Accounts for Small Business
The Crime Writers Casebook
Creative Writing
Freelance Writing
Writing Your own Life Story
Writing performance Poetry
Writing Romantic Fiction
Teaching Your Child to Swim
Creating a Successful Commercial Website
Buying and Selling Online
Buying and Selling Property at Auction
The Straightforward Business Plan
The Straightforward C.V.
Successful Public Speaking
Handling Bereavement
Play the Game-A Compendium of Rules
Individual and Personal Finance

Go to:

www.straightforwardco.co.uk